The Self-Help Guide
for Teens with Dyslexia

of related interest

Can I tell you about Dyslexia?
A guide for friends, family and professionals
Alan M. Hultquist
Illustrated by Bill Tulp
ISBN 978 1 84905 952 7
eISBN 978 0 85700 810 7

Dyslexia and Alternative Therapies
Maria Chivers
ISBN 978 1 84310 378 3
eISBN 978 1 84642 547 9

ALAIS WINTON

The
SELF-HELP GUIDE
for
TEENS
with
DYSLEXIA

Useful Stuff
You May Not Learn at School

Jessica Kingsley *Publishers*
London and Philadelphia

First published in 2015
by Jessica Kingsley Publishers
73 Collier Street
London N1 9BE, UK
and
400 Market Street, Suite 400
Philadelphia, PA 19106, USA

www.jkp.com

Library of Congress Cataloging in Publication Data
Winton, Alais.
The self-help guide for teens with dyslexia : useful
stuff you may not learn at school / Alais Winton.
pages cm
Includes bibliographical references.
ISBN 978-1-84905-649-6 (alk. paper)
1. Dyslexic children--Education. 2. Dyslexics--Education.
3. Learning disabled children--Education. 4.
Learning disabled youth--Education. 5. Reading disability. I. Title.
LC4708.P73 2003
371.9--dc23
2014048997

British Library Cataloguing in Publication Data
A CIP catalogue record for this book is available from the British Library

ISBN 978 1 84905 649 6
eISBN 978 1 78450 144 0

Printed and bound in Great Britain

For Hannah, who gets me, I am
thankful for you every day.

For Gordon, thank you for your love, support,
proofreading skills and so much more.

For Zac and Jacob, I know you have
faced challenges in learning, but I also
know that you will both be amazing
at whatever you choose to do.

Acknowledgements

Many thanks to Mia Broomhall for being my elegant and very patient model. Thanks also to the rest of Broomhall family for their support and encouragement throughout. To Gordon, thanks for proofing my work. Thank you to Mandy and family for their huge support and contributions to the work. Many thanks to Sarah Hoss, for her advice and suggestions, and her unshakeable and continued belief in this idea, even when it was just in my head. Thanks to Hannah Rackham, for being you. Thanks to Jacob Broomhall and Zac Millard for inspiring me to do this. Finally, thanks to everyone else who has helped and supported me in the writing of this book.

Contents

Chapter 1

Welcome to My World

I'd like to start by saying 'hello' to you, whoever you are, reader, and tell you a bit about my story and why I wanted to write this book.

I am dyslexic. You might be dyslexic too or know someone close to you who is, and you probably know what it means to you, but this is what it means for me: I struggle with reading (words often move about on the page, when I'm tired they fall off the end of sentences like lemmings jumping off a cliff and sometimes I don't understand the meaning of what I've read); I often make mistakes in spelling and can't see the mistakes when I look over my work; I lose things and myself easily (even with a satnav!); and I forget things. All of this makes learning harder for me than it would be for someone who doesn't have to cope with this every single day!

On the plus side, I think in three-dimensional images. This means that I can direct a play, make a sculpture or choreograph a group dance entirely in my head. I am creative, intelligent and interested in people – if you happen to have dyslexia, it's vital that you are able to remember the things you are good at when times are tough.

I have spent my life learning. From GCSEs, to a degree and postgraduate certificate in education and, along the way, I have also done courses in belly dancing, car maintenance, basic psychology, beauty therapy, anatomy and physiology and Swedish body massage.

As a college tutor I always promote learning – it can be an amazing experience and can sometimes open unexpected doors – but as a dyslexic there have been times, even as an adult, when the act of trying to learn has reduced me to tears or feelings of anger and frustration. Contained within this book is a collection of ideas and techniques that I have used to help me learn. Without these strategies, I would not have completed my degree in Theatre Studies and English, and subsequent learning would also have been much harder to achieve.

I cannot offer you a cure – if you are dyslexic like me then you will always see things differently – but what I can offer are some solutions to common problems for dyslexics who want to learn. I hope that the suggestions in this book are useful, but most of all I hope that you are able to do whatever you want to do in life and that these tools help you to succeed in the learning you need along the way.

Some of the most successful and inventive people in history and today have found education difficult. Vive le square peg! We should be making the hole a different shape, not the peg! So, the next time your brain is saying 'I don't get it,' that doesn't mean that you won't ever get it, it just means that <u>it</u> isn't being explained in a way that works for <u>you</u>.

Chapter 2

I'm Sure I've Forgotten Something!

If, like me, you forget where you've put things, what you're supposed to be doing and where exactly you're meant to be doing it, then this chapter is for you.

There is nothing quite as infuriating as trying to remember something that you just can't seem to bring to mind, no matter how hard you try. If the thing you want to remember is for an exam, then this becomes not only frustrating, but stressful as well, and is likely to affect your result. You might also end up mentally kicking yourself when you realise that you knew the answer but just couldn't remember it; sadly exams don't usually have an 'ask me later' box to tick.

In order to talk about ways to improve your memory, I first need to explain a bit about memory and how it works in the human brain. You probably already know that there are two different types of memory – long-term and short-term, for example:

- long-term – I remember falling in the pond in school, when I was seven, and going through a phase of drawing and painting purple mountains

- short-term – I remember what I had for breakfast this morning (this is not always the case!).

Learning something while we are actually doing it has to, by its nature, involve short-term memory. Unfortunately, this is the type that I, and most dyslexics, have difficulty with. I can remember the smell of a wood that I haven't been to for at least 20 years, but I sometimes find it difficult to remember something I was told five minutes ago. Part of this is because sensory memory is stronger, but most college courses won't be taught through the medium of smell (aromatherapy may be a rare exception!).

The average person can retain seven items in their short-term memory (five items if their memory is below average and ten if it is above average). The problem is that this could be seven sentences or one seven-digit number, depending on the circumstances. The parts of your brain that deal with memory are the hippocampus and the amygdala.

Imagine that you are the hippocampus and it's your birthday, so you are going to a party where you, quite rightly, expect to be given cards and presents. Your best friend is the amygdala and she loves a party – anything fun and exciting and she wants to be part of it – so she goes with you and at the end of the night helps you carry all your presents and cards home. This is good news, because there were a lot of presents and you wouldn't have been able to manage them all on your own.

The next day you have to go to work and you are expecting more presents and cards, as many of the people you work with couldn't make it to your party. So you text the amygdala to come and help you carry stuff, but she says that work is boring. It's no fun, so she can't be bothered. She has another party to go to, anyway.

So you go on your own but you can't carry everything – it's too much – so you have to leave some things at work, and the next day they have been lost or stolen.

The presents and cards represent the things you need to remember to succeed in learning and without fun and excitement. The amygdala is leaving the hippocampus to his own devices, but unfortunately he can only retain a set amount and once he's full up, anything new that's added will spill over and be left behind – like a glass of water – or will displace something he had already been given.

So, finding the fun in your learning is key to remembering. This isn't always immediately apparent in traditional styles of education, so I have adopted a couple of strategies to help me remember things. I suggest that you use the one that helps you the most or that you can have the most fun with.

The first idea, known as a 'memory palace' (Foer 2011), is to locate information or items in space. This can be very good if you think in pictures. It is very easy to find out if you think in pictures – you simply think of a word – 'tree' for example – and if an image of a tree, rather than the word 'tree' itself, pops into your head, then you probably think in pictures. Whatever you need to remember can be placed in your mind's eye in familiar locations. This could be the rooms of your house, for instance, or your journey to school/college (this is best if you walk and there are landmarks on the way, e.g. a letterbox).

Simply think of the list of things or words that you want to remember and imagine them in key locations. If, for example, you wanted to remember the planets of the solar system, you would imagine Mercury in the middle of your front door, then Venus on something in your hallway (a mirror or picture, perhaps).

You could then imagine yourself walking into the front room and seeing a globe of the Earth, then walking into the kitchen and seeing Mars on the cooker, Jupiter on the stairs, and so on, until you have placed all eight planets in order around your virtual home. Then, whenever you need to call them to mind, you simply mentally retrace your route.

According to legend, this way of remembering by imagining people, objects and so on in a particular space, began with the poet Simonides of Ceos, as he used this technique to remember those whose lives had been lost in the great banquet hall of Thessaly.

This idea of locating items or objects in a familiar location, in combination with the inclusion of multisensory information (e.g. the taste, smell or feel of an item to be remembered) and the characterisation of objects or items to be remembered – in other words instilling objects or words with more meaning and personification (e.g. Mars as an angry planet) – make up the techniques used by the majority of mental athletes who compete in national and international memory championships (Foer 2011).

The second method is to use the information that you need to remember to create a story. For example, if you need to remember the first eight elements of the periodic table, you could use the elements to create a story.

My story would run something like this: a mum called Hydrogen is turning on a tap in her kitchen but nothing comes out (this would remind me that hydrogen comes from the Greek word hydro meaning water, but is actually a colourless gas).

Her daughter, Helium, then comes into the room. She is carrying a balloon shaped like the sun because it is her second birthday (this would remind me that the word helium comes from the word helios meaning sun, is used amongst other things to fill balloons and is the second element in the table).

Helium has a new toy but it needs batteries, so her mother looks in the draw for some lithium batteries (this would remind me of a use for lithium).

Helium's new toy, Beryllium, is a space shuttle, which her mum says she must not put in her mouth because it is poisonous (this would remind me that beryllium can be used in the making of space shuttles and aircraft and is toxic).

Helium's granddad, Boron, then arrives and says that he would like to give her the bumps but his joints are aching because of his arthritis (this would remind me that boron is currently being evaluated for the treatment of arthritis).

Granddad Boron has brought his granddaughter a card with six diamonds on it (this would remind me of the sixth element – carbon, the element from which diamonds are made).

Her mum then accidentally burns her daughter's birthday cake which has 'Nitrogen' written on it (this would remind me that nitrogen can be found in foods and has also been described as 'burnt air').

Finally, the birthday girl has to take eight deep breaths of oxygen to blow out her candles (reminding me of oxygen's main function and that it is the eighth element on the periodic table).

Linguistic mnemonics (systems where each word of a phrase is replaced with another word starting with the same letter) can be a distraction, and less helpful for a dyslexic learner, since they use words rather than images or visual information or narrative. For example, Richard Of York Gave Battle In Vain is commonly used to remember the colours of the rainbow – Red, Orange, Yellow, Green, Blue, Indigo and Violet). Instead, locating items in space using the mind's eye and creating narrative appeal to parts of the brain that are typically stronger in dyslexic learners.

The two methods described above can be useful when you need to remember specific information, for a test or exam, for instance; however, it can be useful to train your memory in a more general way.

This can be done by playing games like Pairs, which help to improve memory. You can search online to find free Pairs games to play.

Or you could play with Snap cards (images) or a standard deck of cards.

To play Pairs, you simply shuffle the pack of cards and then spread them out, face down, on the floor or a table. You then select two cards per go and, if they match, you keep them as a pair. If they don't match, then you place them back face down where you took them from. You can play with other people (the one with the most pairs at the end of the game wins), or on your own – you could time yourself to see how long it takes you to find all the pairs. The key is to remember where you returned certain cards to, so if you pick up a matching card later on, you will know where its matching pair is, even if that card had been turned face up several turns previously. Although there is a degree of randomness to the game (you could turn over a pair on your first go without knowing it was a pair), over time there should be an improvement in memory function as a result of regular use of the parts of the brain that deal with memory.

You can search online to find memory games that you can play for free. Examples of games are: Find the Suspect: the aim of this game is to remember what the 'criminal' looks like and click on the face that was blanked out. This gets harder as more potential 'criminals' are displayed each time; Path Memory: this involves remembering pathways between houses and the order they were shown in; and Blind Spot: in which the player has to remember the original location of objects which have disappeared.

To find more games, you could check out the Dress Up Gal website.[1] These games include a range of Pairs games with different themes (e.g. Halloween). There is also a timed memorising and matching outfits game and a matching hair and makeup game, in which you recreate the look that you were shown at the start.

When talking about memory, the phrase 'use it or lose it' is often quoted, suggesting that,

---

1   www.dressupgal.com.

as humans, the more we 'work' or challenge our memory, the better it will be. A variety of studies have indicated that individuals who regularly complete puzzles, crosswords or similar activities are likely to perform better in memory tests, so it is worth finding some memory games that you enjoy.

Chapter 3

Has Anyone Seen My Phone, and What am I Meant to be Doing Today?

In this chapter I would like to discuss aspects of organisation. I am naturally very disorganised and have had to learn to compensate for this in a number of ways (e.g. I use different colour folders for each unit/subject I teach).

The change that has made the biggest difference to me is about organising stuff, especially at home. I have spent a number of years not knowing where to find such things as keys, money, mobile phone, bank statements and other important items and documentation. If you are anything like me, then I probably don't need to explain the panic and frustration caused by not being able to find my door keys/car keys, etc. when I need to leave the house.

In order to overcome these problems I have had to embrace a system that does not come naturally to me. It is the idea that everything has a place in which it 'lives'.

So, for example, my keys live on a hook on a cupboard door in my kitchen and (as long as have I remembered to return them to where they live!) if I need to find them quickly, I know that that is where they will be.

Important documents (passport, driving licence, etc.) are in a briefcase-style bag, which is always kept in the same place. Any stationery items (stapler, scissors, rulers, etc.) are in the top drawer of the cabinet in the office. And, bizarre as it may sound, the idea that all these items have a 'life' and need somewhere to 'live' makes it easier to keep track of where things are and brings enough order to my chaos for me to be able to function more easily and everyday life to run more smoothly as a result.

Time management is another key part of organisation. It can be very stressful to arrive late for something important, already in a state of upset about being late, and have to find the right room/person, etc. and not know if you have already missed what was happening.

One of my solutions is to allow extra time for journeys, especially journeys that I have never made before. So if it will take me an estimated 30 minutes to drive somewhere, I will allow 45 minutes. This makes the journey much less stressful and allows for unseen hold ups (mostly tractors where I live) but also gives me time to get my bearings when I arrive.

In order to allow more time for journeys, completing tasks and so on, planning ahead is essential. I find calendars/wall charts and diaries very useful for reminding me what is coming up next and in the near future. As I find it difficult to take in large amounts of written text, I tend to just write one or two words on the calendar, which might suggest where I need to be for a meeting (for example St David's) or what I'm doing that day (such as salsa class).

I also like to have two calendars – one for work (kept in the office) and one for social events – friends' birthdays, barbeques or nights out, for example – (kept in the kitchen). That way there isn't too much information on any one day, and I know which calendar to look at if I'm not sure when something is happening.

Diaries can also be very useful, as they are portable. However, I find the pocket-size ones too small to use and, again, it is important for me not to overload pages with too much text – just enough to jog my memory.

With the advancement of technology, mobile phones can be used to set alarms and reminders for meetings or appointments and if the alarm is set a bit earlier than the specified time, it will give you time to get there if you had forgotten about it.

Diaries and calendars can also be handy for highlighting specific blocks of time. For instance, if you have a test or an assignment due in a month's time, and decide you need to work on it for two hours each day, you could block this off each day in green pen. By doing this, you can see quickly when you should be revising or planning, researching and writing your assignment. You could split the two hours into four 30-minute segments with other activities in between to help improve focus and concentration on the task.

Another part of organising work, which is especially useful in learning, is to decide what needs to be done first. This might be really easy to work out. For example, if you are going to have a test on the bones of the hand in the first couple of weeks of your course, you will need to learn this before studying the internal organs of the body. Many courses are separated into different modules and units and within those units the workload is broken down into assignments, tasks, tests and coursework. However, it is useful to break down activities into tasks as small as possible. For instance, 'answer questions on session one hand-out', 'research key terms for session two', 'write introduction to assignment one' and so on.

Making a 'to-do' list is a good way to keep on top of what you need to do. I like to make a to-do list for the day, which has everything on it, from dull household chores to planning teaching sessions and practising salsa steps.

If I don't make a to-do list, I find myself getting easily distracted, sometimes by activities that shouldn't even be on the list! A classic example of this happened yesterday – I walked into town to speak to someone in connection with research for another chapter and, when I finished talking to them, instead of going straight home to continue to work on tasks for the day, I found a sale and did some shopping and as a result got home much later than I expected. If this sort of thing happens once in a while, it might not make much difference, but if it were to occur regularly, or if I have a lot to do, it could have a significant impact on how much work I get done.

If the written part of a to-do list is off-putting, or too time consuming, it is now possible to speak your to-do list into your phone by using the Any.do task and to-do list app.[2] This website contains links for apps that allow you to speak your to-do lists directly into your phone, which then converts your speech into text.

If you have Siri on your phone, you could use this feature, which enables you to create your to-do list and access it later. You will need to enable the feature on your phone to begin with. You can do this using the 'Settings' app and clicking on 'Reminders' and then 'Default list'; this is where reminders will be saved for future use. Next select 'Things', from the main lists view select 'Reminders and Siri' then click on list and select the same one you chose for your default setting. When finished in the top left corner click on 'Settings' and 'Done'. Once you have enabled the feature you can just tell Siri what you want to do and it will automatically be saved as a reminder.

---

2   For more information on this you could check out www.any.do.

When thinking about managing your time it is crucial to be realistic. This is probably one of the most fundamental basics of time management, but it is also the most difficult – how do you know how long something will take if you haven't done it before? So, how do you know if your deadline, whether decided by you or someone else, is realistic and achievable? If you have done a similar task in the past you may have a rough idea of how long it could take, which will be useful, but if it is something new you may have to guess.

My advice would be to allow more time than you think at first. That way, if you finish sooner than expected, you can feel proud of yourself and move on to the next thing, and if it does take longer than you initially thought, it won't be so stressful. Another thing to remember when thinking about being realistic about your use of time is that if you are the kind of person who says 'yes' to everything, you could be taking on too much.

At the start of this chapter I mentioned the fact that I use different coloured folders for each unit or subject I teach. So, for example, my folder for Year Two media is grey and PGCE folders are pink (Year One), purple (Year Two), and so on. If I am studying a course, I try to make the folder even more distinctive (for instance, my anatomy and physiology folder has images of large flamingos).

Colour-coding folders or work may seem a little over the top, but it does help me to locate the right work quickly. If I have a few different resources I need to take to a session, then being able to find the right folder just by searching for a specific colour can make gathering materials together a bit easier and faster.

Finally, don't be afraid to ask for help if you need it. Not just from friends or people in your life who always seem to be super-organised about everything (how do they manage their time and work?), but also, if you know someone who is good at something, can they help you with what you need to do?

When I wanted to run a session about scaling up a Barbie doll to life size, using ratios, before delivering the session for the first time I went to see a tutor who is really good at maths, to make sure I understood the principles and calculations needed. When I needed giant swan-shaped pieces of wood for a play, I asked someone with the right skills to help me. And remember, there will be times when people ask you to help them by doing something that you are good at.

Chapter 4

Picture This

Mind mapping changed my life. That might sound overly dramatic, but it's true. I was 18 and at university and, although I had known for a long time that there was something different about me that made conventional education difficult, I hadn't been diagnosed with dyslexia.

All of the tactics that I had used previously, such as starting work, projects or assignments early, planning ahead, getting written work proofread, etc., were beginning to not be enough to get me through and I was really starting to struggle with both the amount of work and the academic standard required at this level.

Mind maps were invented by Tony Buzan in the 1970s and, although businesses and individuals have been using mind maps for a number of years, it's only really in the last decade that educational establishments in Britain have begun to see the importance of mind maps for learning.

When I was assessed and diagnosed as a dyslexic, the process was commonly known as 'statementing', as it related to being given a statement. A statement is a document provided by a full assessment, carried out by an educational psychologist. In the UK, as of September 2014 this is now known as an Education, Health and Care (EHC) Plan. In the current system, this type of assessment is likely to be a last resort, carried out in the event that initial screening, assessments and interventions, put in place by the school, have been unsuccessful.[3] In the US, the corresponding assessment for dyslexia is known

---

3   Some useful websites on this topic are included in Chapter 11.

as an IEP (Individualized Education Plan) and involves a number of relevant professionals (e.g. education psychologist, teacher, etc).

Under the 'old model', which applied to me, a statement was a fairly standard procedure for identifying dyslexia and it provided access to funding for relevant tools and equipment. As a result of mine, I was given a computer, a portable electronic dictionary and books on mind mapping.

Using mind maps enabled me to take notes quickly, plan assignments and change the structure of assignments before I had written things out in full.

The impact that using mind maps had on my ability to take notes was significant. Like most pupils and students, before the introduction of mind maps I took notes in one of two ways.

The first method was to try to write everything the teacher said as they were saying it. And I do mean everything! I would include 'Good morning', 'and... ', 'but... ', 'because...', etc. I still occasionally come across students who use this method, but I can tell you from bitter experience that it does not work!

It is quite impossible to write down words at the same speed that they are being spoken – this is why journalists still learn how to do shorthand (a system of symbols that allows them to write at the same pace as speech).

With this type of note taking, much of the information will be surplus and probably irrelevant, linking one point to another, for instance. And, crucially, it will be very difficult to take in what is being said if you are busy using your brain to scribble frantically onto paper everything that you are hearing.

The second method was to note down key points. However, this also caused problems – how did I know what the key points were until the end of the class? I would miss important details, or an example given by the teacher that explained the topic clearly but was an addition rather than a key point would not make it into my notes.

Later, when I looked over the notes, I could have no idea what some headings were about or why I decided to include them – so clearly this was not very successful either.

I have found that mind maps allow me to take notes quickly whilst still including a level of detail and being flexible enough to alter them during the session if the emphasis of learning changes.

Prior to the introduction of mind maps, if I had to write an essay or assignment, I would have a only vague idea of what I wanted to write, maybe with some handwritten notes scribbled on a few pages and in no logical order.

I would then start writing on a blank page. I would try to start with an introduction, but within just a few paragraphs I would go off on a tangent and start writing about something vaguely connected but probably not particularly relevant to the topic in question.

I would also often find myself writing about ideas in later paragraphs that would have been better at the start or in the middle of my essay and so would have to write comments like 'as previously discussed', etc. This sort of comment is probably acceptable if used only once or twice in an essay. However, I was often referring back to earlier comments and for me it was an indication that the structure of my written work needed to be improved.

The great thing about mind maps is that they can act as a visual diagram or guide for essays and assignments.

Since I have been using mind maps in this way, I have stopped receiving critical feedback from teachers about the structure of my work and, given that this is an area on which I used to get a lot of negative comments from anyone marking my work, this strategy has obviously helped me.

Most of all, mind maps have helped a great deal with revision. Exams and tests I have passed using mind maps to aid my revision include: English and theatre studies exams at university, theory and practical driving tests and exams in beauty therapy. If I had not passed any of the above, my life would have taken a different turn in terms of my career, and not being able to drive in a relatively rural area would have affected job opportunities as well as my social life.

I really struggled to revise for my GCSEs – I spent hour upon hour in my room desperately trying to will the information into my brain. I stopped seeing my friends and spent most of the time feeling unhappy, worried and stressed.

Although I somehow managed to pass most of my school exams, I didn't feel that they, in any way, reflected what I might actually be capable of. Indeed, the whole experience was so stressful that it put me off the idea of exams, to the extent that I deliberately avoided exams in the next stage of my education and chose, instead, to study for a qualification in Performing Arts that was predominantly practical.

Using mind maps to record on paper all the information I might need for a test or exam, and then spending time reviewing my mind maps, has transformed the way I revise for exams, which in turn has altered my approach to exams, improving my results, which has helped my confidence.

How to create a mind map

- Begin with a central image in the middle of the page. Include a topic or subject heading within your central image if appropriate (for example, the central image of a football may be self-evident, whereas the image of a book may need more clarification – poetry, novels, etc.).

- Once you have created a central image, draw curved lines 'radiating' out from the central image and write subheadings or sub-topics on these lines.

- Each subheading can then be divided again into smaller curved lines (branches), which contain words linking to each topic.

Points to remember when creating a mind map

- A mind map can be any size. I prefer A4 when taking notes and A3 for revision.

- Use a landscape (horizontal) page. This can prevent cluttering and make the map easier to design and read.

- Make your mind map as colourful as possible – colour stimulates the human brain and assists memory. Some parts of the map could be assigned specific colours (e.g. bones of the wrist in green) – this can also speed up information retrieval and recall.

- Use printed words (rather than joined-up handwriting), as printed words have a more definite shape and can be easier to read and remember.

Example mind maps are included at the end of this chapter, and you can find a video on how to mind map by Tony Buzan by searching for 'Maximize the Power of Your Brain – Tony Buzan' on YouTube.

Mind maps can be created by hand or by using mind-map-specific software, of which iMindMap8 is currently the most up to date (as of writing in November 2014). Alternatively, you could try using Coggle software. The Coggle website[4] has an online tutorial on how to use Coggle and the option to sign up to download the software for free.

Case study

Michael and Sandra (I have changed the names to protect their identities) are brother and sister. Their mother asked me to meet them and talk to them about mind maps.

Michael is 14 and has been identified as having dyslexia/dyslexic tendencies at school. He is about to start working towards his GCSEs (High School Diploma in the US), this would mean that he is likely to have a difficult couple of years ahead, even if he did not experience the reading, writing and memory difficulties associated with being dyslexic.

So not only will this be a labour-intensive and stressful time for Michael, but his results may impact greatly on what he wants to do next — both A Levels and National Diploma courses

---

4   This is available at www.coggle.it.

(Advanced Placement Examinations in the US) will require that he attains a certain number of GCSEs at grade C or above.

Michael's sister, Sandra, is two years younger than him and has not exhibited any symptoms that might indicate dyslexia. On first meeting, both Michael and Sandra were very polite and friendly, and Sandra seemed organised when we talked about school and appeared to enjoy being organised and well prepared. Her handwriting was neat and tidy, which can be seen on her mind map on page 51.

I interviewed Michael and Sandra before we discussed mind maps and Michael told me that his favourite subject at school was physical education (PE). When I asked him why this was his favourite subject, he replied, 'I like practical lessons, I don't like writing as much.' I was not surprised by his response — as human beings, we tend to enjoy the things that we are good at more than anything that we may struggle with. Although this is a natural reaction, it also means that in the process of learning we usually improve in the subjects that we already started out being good at because we get pleasure from them, and so we put in more time and effort. Meanwhile, we continue to struggle with subjects or tasks we found difficult in the first place.

I asked Michael and Sandra about their worst or least liked subjects at school. Sandra, whilst enjoying art, said she did not like PE. When asked why this was the case, she responded, 'Because I'm not good at it,' suggesting again that it is difficult to like something we don't feel 'good at'.

Michael, in contrast, whilst identifying PE as his favourite subject, said that his least favourite subject was French. He said he 'would like more input and support from the teacher,' which suggests that this is a subject in which Michael feels he needs more help.

I asked Michael and Sandra to write something about their least favourite subject on the interview sheet. I told them to take as long as they wanted and to let me know when they thought they had finished. Sandra wrote three points about learning different dances, having an athletics week and the timetable for games sessions.

Michael clearly found this a difficult task and took some time. He then wrote a general point about the usefulness of French as a subject: 'You need French for some companies to actually be considering you for a job.' As I would have expected from a dyslexic learner like myself, Michael exhibited signs of incorrect spelling and poor sentence structure.

At first glance this seems to be an unkind task to have set someone suffering with dyslexia. However, the reason I asked this of Michael was in order to compare the difference between this form of writing and his mind maps. It is also worth remembering that this is the way in which most pupils and students are currently asked to show their learning in schools and colleges across the UK.

I asked Michael and Sandra to draw a mind map on the subject of everything that makes them happy. At first, Sandra was concerned about the quality of her images and the neatness of her map. I explained to her that the image didn't need to be a perfect representation, but it just needed to be clear to her. I also encouraged her to reduce the gaps between words, so that she would be able to see the connection more clearly, and to use more colours to excite her brain. Michael, in contrast, having understood the basic concept of how to create a mind map, needed no guidance or encouragement and, in approximately ten minutes, had produced a beautiful and very detailed map, with lots of images.

The second mind map I asked Michael and Sandra to create was on their least favourite school subject (these mind maps are included at the end of this chapter). Sandra included much more detail in mind-map form than in the points she had written on the interview sheet, but the most notable difference for me was in Michael's mind map. In a very short space of time (the whole session lasted approximately an hour), Michael was able to go from writing one general point about his least favourite subject, to documenting on his mind map famous places in France, commonly used phrases, examples of French food and drink, some basic numbers and examples of French football players. Certainly, if I was Michael's French teacher, I would much rather have his mind map as evidence of his learning than his sentence written in the traditional, linear, black and white way.

When Michael and Sandra reached the end of the autumn term, I asked them to complete a follow-up evaluation form on their use of mind maps after our session. Both gave very positive feedback, stating that they enjoyed making mind maps, and that using mind maps meant it took them less time to revise and plan essays than it would have done prior to using them. Whilst Sandra has only used mind maps on a few occasions since we last met (for writing essays or assignments), Michael has been using mind maps regularly for both essay writing and revision. Both Michael and Sandra think that people between the age of 10 and 14 should find out about mind maps.

I am very excited to find out that Michael is already benefitting from mind mapping techniques. I remember all too well the difficulty and challenges presented by two years of intensive coursework and exams, and I feel that anything that can save Michael time and reduce his stress levels has got to be worth the small amount of input and time it takes to learn how to create and use mind maps.

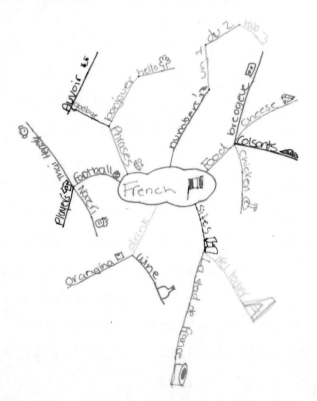

Figure 4.1 Michael's mind map about French

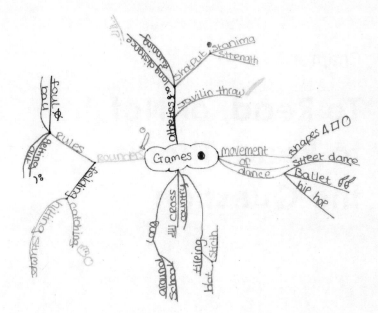

Figure 4.2 Sandra's mind map about PE

Chapter 5

To Read, or Not to Read, That is the Question

This is one of the most important, yet possibly controversial, chapters. Although it is now widely acknowledged that someone who is dyslexic will find reading difficult, there is still a requirement in virtually every educational environment and job to be able to read. The amount of information in written format may vary depending on level and subject; however, even the most practical courses (hair and beauty, motor vehicles, etc.) will require that some content be learnt through reading.

I have personally read many books on dance and choreography (both of which are practical subjects) and was required to read about, amongst other things, the combustion engine, for a qualification in car maintenance.

Reading, for me, has been one of the most challenging and yet rewarding experiences I have encountered. We are not born with an innate ability to read. Genetically, we are not pre-programmed to read in the same way that we are for other tasks (e.g. making sense of visual information, etc.). In order to read we have to develop new connections that link different parts of the brain (e.g. the part that deals with recognising visual information needs to link to the part that deals with processing information and the parts that deal with retention, memory, etc.). All of these different parts of the brain must work together to identify individual letters in the alphabet, remember their sounds and then link them together to form words.

Although in some ways English is a less complex language than some previous and

current systems of language (e.g. Chinese),
in that it contains fewer characters (letters)
in the alphabet, it has been complicated by
its influences being derived from previous
languages (e.g. Latin, Greek, French, etc.).
For instance, the silent 'c' in muscle is derived
from the Latin word 'musculus'; this is also
where we get the word 'muscular' from, in
which the letter 'c' is pronounced (Wolf 2008,
p.42). This linguistic trait can be very confusing
for a dyslexic reader, since most dyslexics read
and write using a phonetic (memorised sounds)
system, which does not take into account the
idiosyncrasies (quirks) of the English language.

This again creates a gap between verbal
and written communication for anyone with
dyslexia or dyslexic tendencies. In other words,
what I can convey through speech is clearer
and more articulate than what I can convey
on paper, and also the mechanical process of
reading can be very difficult.

I have come to see the process of reading
as being a bit like learning to drive a car. When
you start to learn to drive (as you will know if

you've done it) you must first of all master the mechanical and practical aspects of driving (how to start the car, change gear, accelerate, brake, etc.). During the process of learning to drive you gradually become less aware of these things and begin to do them in a way that feels automatic. And once you don't need to concentrate on these mechanical functions, you can use your brain for other important aspects of driving (such as looking out for possible hazards, being aware of speed limits, navigation and so on).

A similar process seems to occur with reading for people who are not dyslexic, whereby they can concentrate on the content of what they are reading without having to focus on the mechanics of how they are actually reading.

The act of reading itself poses a number of issues for me. First, if I come across a word I haven't seen written down before, then I may not recognise it and therefore am unlikely to understand the meaning of the word.

There is also the problem that words can appear to be moving around on the page. This occurs as a result of Irlen Syndrome. Irlen Syndrome is not dyslexia but is frequently linked to it (as it can occur at the same time) and, in my case, means that, especially if I'm reading when I'm tired, words seem to fall off the ends of sentences. For some people the words jump around on the page, making reading incredibly challenging.

Then there is also the problem of meaning. I can often read a paragraph and get to the end of it and find that either I have been thinking about something else and have no idea what I've just read or, whilst having <u>read</u> the words, I did not actually <u>understand</u> the meaning behind them. This means that I will have to reread sections of a book, sometimes several times, until I am happy that I have taken in and understood what has been written – this can be very time consuming.

These difficulties in reading can be dealt with in different ways depending on your budget and your confidence in the use of technology.

The first issue is that of encountering an unrecognised word. This can be addressed by highlighting the word (if the book belongs to you) and then typing it into a computer and looking it up using the thesaurus option in Word or an online dictionary. Alternatively, you could use an electronic reading pen to record the word and store it until you can plug the device into a computer and look it up – this avoids having to find the word at a later date and copy it correctly. An electronic reading pen (C-Pen 3.5 USB digital highlighter) or Quicktionary 2 (which scans and provides a definition of the word on a small built-in screen) can be purchased easily online, however these options are not cheap (£80–£125 at the time of writing).

The second problem (words moving around the page) can be greatly reduced by changing the background colour of the page. This procedure is quite straightforward on a PC or Apple Mac (in Microsoft Word there should be an option to change the page colour in the 'layout' or 'page layout' menu). Some Kindles have the option to change the background colour. Alternatively, if you are reading something in a printed format, a coloured reading ruler can be useful. These can be bought in one colour or as a variety pack from Crossbow Education.[5]

Changing the background colour from white to another colour has the effect of anchoring the words to the page and can make them easier to read. Everyone's colour preference seems to be different, so it's important to experiment until you find one that works for you (bright yellow seems to work best for me).

The Dyslexia Research Trust has carried out investigations into the benefits of using a yellow or blue overlay. Yellow is thought to prevent 'whiteout', a scenario in which it is difficult to make out individual shapes due to an excess of white, which is why skiers often

---

5 Available at www.crossboweducation.com and www.crossboweducation.us.

wear yellow goggles. Yellow is a good colour for improving outline definition, which helps to enhance the sharpness of black text and make it stand out more against a yellow background. Blue is believed to connect with the parts of the brain that are linked to concentration. A study carried out by the Dyslexia Research Trust on dyslexic children who wore blue filters for three months showed a significant improvement in their reading ability (Dyslexia Research Trust n.d.).

The Dyslexia Research Trust suggests that yellow and blue are the only colours that will have an impact on visual disturbances in reading. However, my local optician (part of a larger national chain) uses an 'intuitive colorimeter' chart, provided by Cerium Visual Technologies, to assess young people with visual disturbances linked to reading, and provides the appropriate tinted lenses if improvements using the overlays have been identified. General eyesight and other eye conditions would be eliminated prior to this intervention. However, if you suffer from visual disturbances when reading, it is worth visiting an optician. Remember, all eye treatment in the UK is free to anyone under the age of 16, however, if you are anywhere else in the world it is worth checking whether this is the case for you.

If you think that you may have Irlen Syndrome, which can affect how you see words on the page and cause other visual disturbances, you can find out more online[6] and could investigate glasses with tinted lenses as an option to minimise the symptoms of the syndrome.[7] Many books are also now printed in a large-text format, which might be helpful for some readers.

The last issue – difficulty understanding the meaning of what has been read – is common for many dyslexics. Getting a second opinion (e.g. from a friend or family member or

---

6   See www.irlen.org.uk.

7   To test yourself for Irlen Syndrome, and the location of contact centres in the UK, visit www.irlenuk.com and Irlen.com for the US.

member of a learning support team if you have access to one) is useful, but it may not always be possible or practical. You could also use software called Read&Write Gold (currently on version 10).

Reading and writing using Read&Write Gold

Read&Write Gold provides a toolbar that can be used with other applications (e.g. Microsoft Word), which allows you to listen to what you have written or scanned (you will need headphones or speakers). The toolbar also includes an enhanced spellcheck feature, a word prediction feature and a folder that can save websites that you have looked at when researching something – creating an automatic bibliography. You can find out more and purchase Read&Write Gold from the Texthelp website.[8]

Your computer will need a certain amount of memory (RAM) and free disk space to run

---

8   See www.texthelp.com.

the programme, so you will need to check that these requirements are met before purchase. Some educational institutions may have a site licence for this software, so this may be another way to access it if, for any reason, you are unable to use it at home.

One of the reasons why this software is so useful for the dyslexic learner is that it was developed in partnership with Kent Fire and Rescue Service specifically to assist employees with dyslexia.

The story began with an individual who eventually joined Kent Fire and Rescue Service, following four unsuccessful attempts to pass the entrance exam. He went on to become Chair of the Service's Dyslexia Group and, in 2006, Kent Fire and Rescue Service approached Texthelp and, following evaluation, Read&Write software was made available on every PC and laptop owned by the Service in 2007.

Although this example is specific to employment, I believe that this software is vital in education to support learners with reading difficulties, whether they are dyslexic or find reading challenging for other reasons.

So, returning to the original question of this chapter, 'To read, or not to read, that is the question', I would always encourage reading, no matter how difficult or time consuming the act of reading itself might be. In my early teens I read very little and not very often; now I am an avid reader – I read every night and I can quite happily devour a good book in less than a week, something I never thought possible at an earlier age.

So, what changed? Well, I was lucky enough to meet someone with a keen interest in books and a large collection of them. Because the process of reading is not easy for me, I have to decide, first and foremost, if a book is going to be worth the time and effort I know I must dedicate to it. So, personal recommendations are really useful and, if the person recommending the book can also tell you a bit about it, then so much the better. The back cover should provide some information (review extracts and the blurb, etc.). However, reviews extracts can be misleading – '...hilarious...' might in its full context actually say: 'This book is the least hilarious thing I have ever read' – and blurbs can be deliberately cryptic or lengthy, which is unhelpful if you then decide the book is not for you.

To conclude, reading has given me more than it has taken (in time and concentration, etc.). It has given me some sense of the grammatical and stylistic elements of the written word, a wider vocabulary by introducing me to new words and an opportunity to escape into realms and ideas beyond my own imagining. So, whilst I will always be aware of the process of reading, and may have to reread certain passages and, perhaps, identify the meanings of unfamiliar words, this doesn't stop me from enjoying good books.

Chapter 6

What Does This Mean?

I have already touched on the idea of understanding meaning in the previous chapter, but this is such a significant topic that I feel it deserves a chapter of its own. I will attempt to explain why by recounting a true story, which highlights how important it is to understand the meaning of what you are being asked to do in education, and just how easily things can go astray when you don't understand what is being asked.

I was in my first year at university and, although I had struggled with school and college, I had not yet been officially diagnosed as having dyslexia (that occurred at the start of my second year at university). The coping techniques that I had been using, such as giving myself more time to do essays or assignments, starting work as soon as the task was given out and reading only relevant chapters etc., were beginning not to be anywhere enough to support me at this level of education.

My class was asked to write an assignment about visiting artists, so off I went and researched visiting artists, planned and wrote the essay and submitted it to the tutor.

The next week the tutor asked to see me and explained that, whilst I had written a good assignment, I had written about the wrong thing. It turned out that everyone else had written about artists visiting and performing in Wales, whereas I had written about a Welsh performance group which visited other countries and, whilst the tutor in question was sympathetic and supportive, my assignment did not meet the requirements of the grading criteria and, therefore, could not be marked. I had to resubmit this assignment.

Looking back, had I asked questions or had a ten-minute conversation with the tutor to check what was being asked for, I could have saved myself hours of additional work.

At the time I was embarrassed and confused. How come everyone else seemed to understand and I didn't? Since then, I have realised three things that have changed my outlook and behaviour.

First, due to my dyslexia, my brain operates in a fundamentally different way to non-dyslexics, so some things are bound to get 'lost in translation'.

Second, there is no such thing as a stupid question. All questions are about inquisition and curiosity and without these key traits of human nature, we would never have become the developed, civilised societies that exist today.

And, finally, when you ask a question, especially in a learning environment, there is a very good chance that at least one other person wanted to ask that same question. Or someone else is waiting for the confidence and opportunity to ask their own question. By asking the first question, you may have 'opened the flood gates' and started a question and answer section within the class that will ultimately help learners to have a deeper understanding of the content being taught.

Of course, questioning works best if the instructions are spoken and you have contact with the person giving them. But what if the instructions or task are given in a written format, for instance a hand-out or a document placed on a shared computer site?

As previously discussed, the act of reading can be a disorientating and difficult process for someone with dyslexic tendencies. Not only is it the case that words may appear to move on the page for some people, but some words may also appear to be missing altogether and this can have a huge impact on meaning. For example, the sentences 'No need to shop' and 'Need to shop' have opposing meanings depending upon whether the word 'No' is included or not.

To try to reduce the frequency of this happening you could consider some of the suggestions from the previous chapter, for instance using software such as Read&Write Gold.

However, there is also a technique designed to improve the understanding of meaning for dyslexic readers suggested by Ronald D. Davis in his book *The Gift of Dyslexia* (1994). He recommends that whenever the reader arrives at some punctuation in the text (commas, full stops, brackets, and so on), they try to form a mental picture or feeling about what they have just read.

I started using this basic system in 1995, not long after my introduction to it, and since then I have been able to extend it to using the technique at the end of sentences and now at the end of every paragraph. I will ask myself: do I understand what I just read? Can I visualise images that represent the text, or do I feel a certain way about what I've just read? Did it make me feel sad or angry? I will also try to summarise in my head, so I think about what I would say if I was going to tell someone else about the paragraph.

If I cannot answer any of these questions for myself, then I know I have not 'taken it in', or understood the meaning of the words. I have been distracted by their shape and not made the connections I needed to in order to perceive the meaning. If this is the case, then I have to read the paragraph again. This is why it is a good idea to start with very small sections of the text, as it is less to reread, if that is what needs to be done.

The above strategy will work for most books and magazines; however, it cannot be applied to forms. We live in an age where you need a form for just about anything – college applications, getting a passport or driving licence, the electoral roll and much more. Some people like filling in forms, but I can quite definitely say that I am not one of those people.

The combination of tiny writing, which makes it difficult for me to read, and needing to follow very specific instructions in a set order (use black ink only, put an X not a tick in the box, and so on) can still reduce me to tears.

My best friend, who, like me, is dyslexic, is an intelligent, creative and professional woman, who is always working at least two jobs and is also a mother. I admire her immensely for all this and more, and yet, on more than one occasion, she has spoken to me about the stress she feels about having to fill in some form or other.

The most recent form I had to fill in, for a renewal of my driving licence, included a stipulation that my signature did not extend beyond the box provided, presumably so that it can be read by a computer. However, as a human being, it would be very easy to mess this up and have to start again.

Unfortunately, my advice on form filling is limited. The only way that I have found to deal with this particular issue is to involve other people. This might be someone close to you who is willing and able to help or the organisations themselves.

Staff at the post office have always been willing to check any forms that go through them, and I have, on occasion, phoned organisations (for example the tax office, my local council and so on) to request giving my answers over the phone so that a member of staff can fill it in on my behalf.

Sadly, until Western society becomes less bureaucratic, dyslexics will have to rely on the support and help of others. Using an online option does mean that software such as the Read&Write Gold toolbar could be of some help and that changes or corrections can be made more easily than with a paper copy.

Chapter 7

I Don't Even Know Which Letter it Starts With

Although most people might consider spelling difficulties to be the most well-known aspect of thinking and learning that impacts on someone who is dyslexic, I, personally, do not believe that this is the most detrimental element of being dyslexic, which is why I have not talked about spelling until now.

However, it is important to include a chapter on this, as I was reminded recently, when chatting to the parent of a teenage dyslexic, what a pain spelling can be.

The parent was relating the story of how her child had not known how to spell a word and had been told by the teacher to 'Just look it up!' This was an all too familiar phrase to me, but, like the child in question, I was often unable to 'just look up' a word in a dictionary, as I wouldn't know where to begin. If you don't even know the correct first letter of the word and are not sure of the correct order of the alphabet then looking something up could be a 'mission impossible'.

There are many words in the English language that start with letters that differ from the sound of the word. For instance, the word 'immense' always sounds to me as if it should begin with an 'e', and 'ph' can often replace an 'f' sound in words such as 'pharmacy', 'phantom', etc. If you were to ask someone whose reading and writing is based on a phonetic system to look up these words, they might spend a long time searching the 'f' section of the dictionary.

When I ask newly arrived students to write something for the first time, the most common complaint is that they are worried about their spelling, whereas what I actually want to see is if they have any understanding of the subject or content of what we have been doing. To some teachers and members of government education departments, this lack of concern for correct spelling may be viewed as a kind of heresy in light of the recent push to improve literacy standards in the UK.

However, technology can be used to correct spelling. So, if like me, you find spelling difficult, it isn't actually the end of the world, but if my students are struggling at the start to understand content, then we have a far greater challenge on our hands than finding ways to correct spelling mistakes.

Ronald D. Davis suggests a 'speak and spell' method (Davis 1994), whereby the dyslexic learner spells out a word, letter by letter, the teacher or parent says the word and then the learner repeats it, (unless the learner thinks they can guess the word, in which case they can say it as soon as they have finished spelling it).

This method might work for some younger learners. However, it needs the involvement of more than one person and also requires a great deal of patience and concentration on the part of the learner. Hence, Davis recommends it only be carried out for a maximum of ten minutes at any one time.

Personally, I have come to accept that I am never going to win any prizes for my spelling and will always make mistakes – I was once made to stand on my chair for an hour in front of the class because I did so badly in a spelling test in school. As a teacher, I rely heavily on technology to reduce the number of spelling errors in my work.

Most people are familiar with the spellchecker function of Microsoft Word (underlining the misspelled word in red and offering you a drop-down menu of the most likely alternative options). I use this in conjunction with the thesaurus option to check that I have made the correct selection from the drop-down menu if I am unsure which word I need. 'Affect' and 'effect' are typical examples of words I might check, as the words are so similar in sound and structure, that I'm never sure, without checking, which one I want to use.

Occasionally, the spellchecker is baffled by my attempt at spelling a word and offers no suggestions; in this instance, links to an online dictionary or proofreader can be useful.

Another feature I find useful in Word is the contextual spellchecker. This is really helpful for me, and it has improved the work of some of the dyslexic learners I have worked with, as this was previously a way in which many dyslexic learners might get caught out. This is to do with words that sound the same but are spelt differently and have different meanings. For example 'where' and 'wear', 'two', 'to' and 'too', etc. The contextual spellchecker works in a similar way to the standard one – it underlines the word in blue instead of red, but still has the drop-down menu of alternatives.

This feature, although very useful, can have unpredictable results. I just tried two examples, deliberately using a word in the wrong context. The contextual spellchecker picked up on one example, but not the other. It also uses quite a bit of computer memory, so it needs to be activated in Microsoft Word 2013: click on 'File', then 'Options' ('Options' at the bottom of the 'File' dropdown menu), then 'Proofing' in the right-hand toolbar and then the 'Use contextual spelling' option. Apple Mac computers have this feature automatically, so it doesn't need to be activated if you are working on one.

You can also set most modern computers to change certain words for you as a default whilst you are writing. This can be helpful if there are certain words that you find yourself misspelling on a regular basis; 'equipment' and 'tomorrow' are examples of words I will misspell nine times out of ten.

As my brain is geared towards thinking pictorially and in three dimensions, it can sometimes help to reinforce the spelling of a word by creating it in a three-dimensional way. For instance, making the word out of clay or using alphabet sets of 'wet and stick' letters, as these letters are colourful, three-dimensional and have an interesting textured surface on one side (and they don't have to be used in a bathroom but can be arranged on a table or similar flat surface).

Word games

Unlike some people, I don't believe that word games should be avoided if you are dyslexic, in the same way that I don't believe reading should be avoided. Whilst there is no magic cure for dyslexia, playing games that involve the construction of words and the ability to spell can bring improvements over time.

I played Scrabble with my family quite often as a child and, although I was inevitably poor at it (quite spectacularly poor on occasion!), it broadened my vocabulary by introducing me to new words and making me think about how words were spelled. Although you might need to adopt a philosophical approach to not being the likely champion in a game of Scrabble, the greater the exposure to different words, the more likely you are to master them.

A game of Scrabble no longer needs to involve other people either. It can be played online independently, or if you want to play against other people virtually online, you can do this by joining certain sites as a member.

I bought my friend's dyslexic son a word game as a present to play with his friends (a card version of Pass the Bomb) and, even though it caused some raised eyebrows amongst the adults about its potential suitability, once I had explained the rules to him, he was quite happy to go and try it. Instructions on how to play Pass the Bomb and sites on which to play this can be found online; see the resources list at the end of the book for more information and web addresses.

Boggle is one of my favourite word games, as it is quick and easy to play. You have a grid into which fit cube-shaped letters (with a different letter on each side of the cube) and a plastic transparent lid. You begin by shaking the letters to form random formations. The timer is then set and players try to create as many words as possible using letters that are next to each other (horizontally, vertically or diagonally) within the time limit. The longer the word, the more points it scores. This game can also be played online.

Again, the key to encouraging learning to occur is enjoyment. So the more entertaining you find the game (even if it is also challenging at first), the more likely that learning will take place. This could happen without the players even realising that they are learning, as well as having a fun experience.

Chapter 8

A Word on Numbers

I suppose I should start this chapter by saying something about when and where numbers and counting began. Then, if you are finding numbers a challenge, at least you will know whom to blame.

Numbers and counting originated in Sumer (a very early civilisation located in what is now the Middle East). It is believed that in Sumeria, in about 4000 BC, numbers and counting were introduced to keep account of animals, crops and goods for the purpose of trading, or the buying and selling of goods.

To begin with, people were given tokens to represent what they had. So, for example, if you had three chickens you would be given three tokens. These tokens later became marks on a sort of clay tablet – so, again, three chickens equals three marks.

In order to stop people from lying and just putting as many marks as they liked (suggesting that they had more chickens/ goods than they really did), these marks were checked and validated by a group of people (the first accountants) who would then give an official stamp to show the marks were a true representation of what that person had (Law 2012).

Some dyslexic and non-dyslexic learners have difficulties understanding number sequences, memorising numbers and gaining arithmetic skills; these difficulties are part of a learning difficulty known as 'dyscalculia'.

Dyscalculia has been described as the numerical equivalent of dyslexia. It is possible to have dyscalculia and not dyslexia or to have dyslexia without dyscalculia (40–50% of dyslexics researched showed no signs of dyscalculia (British Dyslexia Association n.d.)).

A small percentage of the population (3–6%) have been identified as having dyscalculia in isolation. However, studies have only been carried out on children (there is little or no data currently available on adults with dyscalculia) and these children had excellent performance in other aspects of learning (British Dyslexia Association n.d.).

If you think you may have dyscalculia, or you just find numbers a bit of a minefield, then this chapter is for you.

I have never been identified as having dyscalculia (unbelievably, there is still no formal test for this learning difficulty) and, in comparison with dyslexia, very little research seems to have been carried out on this subject.

I used to think that my own relationship with numbers and mathematical ability was somewhat unusual, because at school I could often come up with the correct answer, or end result, with absolutely no idea how I got there or what mental calculations I should have carried out to reach the correct conclusion. As an adult, I am beginning to think that this may be less odd, as I have met other people who have had the same experience as me.

As with other chapters, there is no 'cure' – no magic wand – to rid you of difficulties with numerical data and calculations and the frustrations this might cause in learning and in everyday life. All I can offer are ideas for supporting your learning, alternatives to traditional methods and the sincere hope that the suggestions may be of use to you.

Remembering numbers in the correct order seems to be a good place to start, as this skill might be needed for many mathematical activities: addition, subtraction, multiplication, algebraic formula, etc. These two sequences of numbers '11092001' and '31081997' may seem meaningless and impossible to remember. However, if you split them up into 11/09/2001 and 31/08/1997 and realise their significance (the day that the twin towers were attacked in New York and the day Princess Diana died), they suddenly take on meaning and become representative of two of the most memorable days for any Western person alive at the time.

We think about numbers all the time: birthdays, important anniversaries, telephone numbers, bus numbers, car number plates, pin numbers, etc. So, when confronted with a sequence of numbers, I try to break it down and attach meaning to the numbers.

Another way to remember numbers is called 'The Major System', invented by Johann Winkelmann (a surname we probably <u>will</u> remember!) in the seventeenth century. This system is basically the idea that numbers are converted into a code of letters and phonetic sounds, which can then become words or images and be remembered using the 'memory palace' (see Chapter 2). For example, if the number two is represented by the letter 'N', and the number four is represented by the letter 'R', then 42 (RN) might be remembered as RuN. And so, whenever the numbers appear in that order, you could imagine someone running. As long as all the numbers from zero to nine are covered, you could even invent your own special code (let me know if you come up with a really good one).

If words as well as numbers can be problematic, the above 'system' may just switch one set of incomprehensible information for another. So, if you enjoy practical or movement activities, you could swap the numbers for movements.

I recently spent a very enjoyable 45 minutes teaching a very talented young lady the numbers one to nine in movement form (see Figure 8.1 on the next page), from which I was then able to teach her the prime numbers (a number divisible only by itself and one) between 0 and 100. In order to achieve a two-digit number (e.g. 37), we simply combined two movements (three and seven) together. The possibilities are endless with this technique.

Figure 8.1 Learning numbers through movement

I have based the movements I used on ballet and contemporary dance, as that is my own background, but you could use any form of movement that suits you (e.g. t'ai chi, karate, hip hop, etc).

Movement can be a really useful way to learn. You have probably heard the term 'muscle memory' – this doesn't mean that the muscles themselves are remembering, but that when we repeat movements a specific part of our brain is engaged, which helps the action to become unconscious, (so we can do it without being aware of thinking about it).

So, for example, most people learn to ride a bike when they are quite young, and learning this for the first time may take some time and involve lots of concentration on the actions needed to ride. But, once learned, it will be possible to ride a bike without thinking about what you need to do (pedal, balance, steer, etc.). If years pass without riding a bike and you then return to it, you will remember how to do it and will not need to relearn it.

Riding a bike has to be learned through movement because it is a practical hands-on activity, but if you are prepared to 'think outside the box', or dare to be different, you can learn almost anything you want through movement, including prime numbers (see Figure 8.1).

However, when it comes to maths, numbers are just one part of the equation (deliberate maths pun!). Formulae for calculations also need to be remembered. Even if you don't have dyscalculia, this can be tricky for anyone with dyslexia who, like me, finds sequences difficult. If I store my folders at home in the wrong order, as long as I know where each one is, it probably doesn't matter much. However, if I follow mathematical calculations in the wrong order, the answer is likely to be wrong.

You may already have your own way of dealing with this problem (another maths pun – I'm on fire today!), but this is my method: make a note of the steps you need to make a calculation, in the correct order (if it's long-winded or difficult, ask someone good at maths to help – most teachers like to be asked for help as it makes them feel smart and useful). So, for example, the steps needed to work out the percentage of something would be:

1. the number you want to know the percentage of (probably the bigger number)

2. divide by 100

3. multiply the answer by the percentage (e.g. 10 for 10%).

Before carrying out the calculation that I need the answer to (e.g. 16% of 274), I find it useful to start with something straightforward that I already know the answer to – so I can check the steps are correct.

So, for example, I know that 50 per cent of anything is going to be half the number I started with. So, if half of 120 (120 divided by 2) is 60, then 50 per cent of 120 should be 60. So, using 120 as my starting number, I follow the steps above:

- 120

- divided by 100 = 1.2

- then 1.2 × 50 (percentage) = 60.

If you want to practise your mental arithmetic (maths calculations in your head), you could check out a couple of online game sites. I found Batters Up Baseball Math, which combines a baseball game with multiplication or addition in various levels of difficulty, very addictive – although I was unable to hit a 'home run'. I also enjoyed Battlemath, a game which involves quick mental calculations to try and stop your virtual house being set on fire or destroyed by giant bees (what a brilliant idea!).

If all else fails and you have tried everything and are still baffled and bewildered by all things numerical, take consolation in the knowledge that most people who grew up after the advent of the digital calculator (yes, that also includes me!) are probably doing their level best to hide or disguise how bad they are at mental arithmetic – I find distraction techniques (e.g. get people to talk about the weather while you work it out) and lots of smiling is best for this.

Chapter 9

Stress-busting!

The distance between what my brain is capable of (verbal communication, visual imagery, imagination, etc.) and what can be easily transferred to the page varies depending on circumstances and what I am trying to achieve. This gap, which I am usually aware of, causes endless stress and frustration. All of the dyslexics I have met also have an awareness and experience of this difference between what is thought and what can be transmitted in a written format. The pressure to achieve in learning (sometimes created by teachers or parents but also often by ourselves) can make it a stressful and less than enjoyable process. If

I want to do well, this stress seems inevitable. Consequently, I have taken onboard some ideas and techniques for dealing with, and minimising, stress and, although some of the following ideas are quite obvious, it has taken me a long time to apply them to learning.

Boomerang

The first idea seems contrary to what you might naturally assume, so it can be hard to put into practice. If, like me, you are dyslexic or have what have now come to be known as dyslexic tendencies, you will probably have found that any form of written work takes you a lot more time to produce than a non-dyslexic person would take. The idea of taking breaks, then, might seem impossible as you probably feel that you need that time to keep up with everyone else. However, your brain needs regular breaks; especially if you get to a point where you feel as if you are banging your head against a brick wall and cannot overcome the problem that you are stuck on. Problems you are stuck on might include: not knowing quite which word would be most appropriate to use in an assignment/essay; not understanding a particular aspect of the task given; or feeling as if the information that you need in order to be able to revise just isn't sinking in.

I trained in contemporary dance a number of years ago, and my tutor taught me a very valuable lesson, which applies to all subjects, not just dance. If her students were struggling to learn a certain movement, she would ask us, instead of trying to repeat the move over and over, to stop and do something else and return to it later. So I have come to see this as a 'boomerang' theory, as I know I will return to the problem later having taken time out to do, or think about, something else. This space for my brain can often mean the solution is reached subconsciously, when my brain doesn't really even tell me it's sorting it out; this is less stressful than agonising over the problem and getting nowhere.

Exercise

The correlation between exercise and a reduction in stress, predominantly as a result of exercise reducing the amount of cortisol (stress hormone) in the body, has been known for a number of years, to the point where doctors and counsellors will now, in some cases, recommend exercise as a form of treatment for some mental health problems (e.g. mild depression, etc.). What is currently being studied by some scientists and scientific institutions (for example Professor Kramer's work at the University of Illinois and research being carried out at Cambridge University) is the link between exercise and improved brain power and brain function.

These studies examine not only the effect of exercise in preventing dementia in the elderly, but also the impact of aerobic exercise in young people. Professor Kramer has carried out studies that suggest that physically fit and active children are better able to multitask and problem-solve compared with less physically fit children (Gray and Russell 2012). And

Cambridge University has carried out studies that link the act of running to the growth of new brain cells, especially those linked to memory (Sample 2010).

So, whilst I would advocate exercise as a means of de-stressing (hence its presence in this chapter), recent research seems to suggest that it may also be very good for the brain and, therefore, aid learning.

My big confession here is that at school I hated PE classes. In part due to dyspraxic tendencies[9] mixed in with my dyslexia, my hand–eye coordination is truly appalling. This is no exaggeration. In the five years that I was at secondary school, I played rounders every week during the spring and summer terms and never once managed to hit the ball. Even in terms of probability I should have hit it at least once by chance, but I never did. In fact, I was so bad at PE that if I was absent (helping

---

9   Dyspraxia can occur alongside dyslexia and relates to difficulties of spatial awareness and physical coordination. People who have dyspraxia are often mistakenly thought of as being clumsy.

the English/Drama department instead, for instance), my predicted grades were better than the grades I achieved if I actually turned up and participated!

Fortunately, however, things have moved on since I was at school, and PE is no longer limited to rounders, netball and hockey for girls and football, rugby and cricket for boys. As an adult, I have greatly enjoyed classes in t'ai chi, belly dancing, pilates and salsa. The range of exercise options is now so broad and diverse, from snowboarding, hip hop and street dance to parkour and boxercise, that it would be difficult not to find something appealing.

Creativity

Creative activities are also a good way to relax. If your brain works in a predominantly visual way (and this seems to be the case for all the dyslexics I have met), then it is important to make time to indulge and use this aspect of the brain. This could be achieved through painting, drawing, making collages, craft, photography, etc. Or you may prefer a more movement-related creative activity – dancing, acting or singing might be your thing.

Ideally, at least one of these activities should be carried out in a recreational way – solely to give you pleasure – and not be accompanied by any form of testing or criteria. In this way, there is no pressure on you to produce anything of a certain standard. You can simply enjoy doing the activity and being in the moment, instead of worrying about the future – the outcome. What each person chooses will be different. Personally, I enjoy cutting up old cards and postcards and creating a collage, or using silk threads to make friendship bracelets – both are quick, easy, very hands on and use my creative brain (choice of images, colours, etc.).

This idea of being creative links in with the next part of this chapter. It concerns something that may seem so obvious, but I have often forgotten to do it, especially when I have found learning difficult and challenging: remember what you're good at. We all have things that we naturally excel at and other things that we struggle with, and this is never more apparent than in learning.

For instance, in a beauty course that I took recently, I remembered the different massage movements quickly and was able to perform them in the correct order after only a few additional practices at home. However, I struggled to remember the Latin names for the bones in the hands and feet.

It can be very easy to become downhearted when finding an aspect of learning difficult and it can leave you feeling as if you are no good at anything. Now, although I have never met you, I can confidently say that this is absolutely and without doubt not the case. I have worked with students and learners for over ten years, at a variety of ages (eight-year-olds through to mature adults) and levels (from students with serious learning difficulties to postgraduate students), and I have never met a student who wasn't good at something. So, my suggestion, based on my own experience, is, if you don't yet know what it is that you're good at, try everything until you find out. And if you do

know, then remind yourself of all the things
that seem easy to you when you are attempting
to do something that does not come naturally.
Admittedly, it is not always easy to do this;
however, there have been times when trying to
remember what I <u>can</u> do has stopped me from
walking away from an educational experience
and renewed my determination to succeed.

Visualisations

Another technique for reducing stress, which
I encourage my students to use, is positive
visualisation. This often feels a bit strange
the first time you try it, but it can be very
effective. There are a variety of visualisations,
and many books have been published on
the subject. I use two on a regular basis –
one to aid relaxation and one to imagine a
positive outcome.

Relaxation visualisation

Close your eyes. Imagine that you are lying
on soft grass in a clearing in the middle of a
forest. You can feel the luscious soft earth

beneath you. You can smell the spring flowers –
bluebells, primroses, snowdrops and crocuses.
You are surrounded by a circle of trees – they
are protecting you from all outside influences.
You can smell the deep musty scent of the
wood. You can see the clear, blue sky above
you. Now you are transported to a beach; let
your body sink into the warm sand. Gently
wiggle your toes, imagine the sand in between
them. You can hear the gentle lapping of the
waves against the shore. You can see the birds
flying overhead and smell the fresh salty air.
On the shoreline you see a boat. Imagine that
you are sending all your worries and stresses to
the boat. Once you have placed your worries
on the deck of the boat, watch it sail off into
the distance until it is out of sight, taking your
worries with it. You look back up at the sky
and gradually it begins to change; the colours
are transforming – blue into pink, yellow, then
oranges, reds and purples – all the colours
bleeding together in perfect harmony. You
enjoy watching the most beautiful sunset. Take
a few minutes to enjoy the feeling of peace

and when you open your eyes, make sure you get up slowly.

Positive outcome visualisation

This can follow on from the relaxation visualisation or be carried out separately. Start by closing your eyes and focusing on the goal to be achieved (e.g. passing a written exam, passing your driving test, performing on stage or graduating with a degree). Once you have your own goal in mind, imagine that you are at the end of that process, after the performance or exam etc., and that you have been successful. Try to create in your mind's eye a scenario in which you have achieved your goal. For instance, after a successful performance, the audience would applaud and later congratulate you on how well you performed. In the example of the driving test, you could imagine the examiner telling you that you have passed, and for the degree you could imagine your own graduation ceremony; the more detail that you can include (the colour of your graduation gown, for instance), the better. Once you have envisaged a positive outcome, try to connect to how that successful achievement makes you feel and keep this feeling with you when you open your eyes.

If you begin an exam or performance with a positive mindset, it can affect the outcome. The more relaxed and happy you can be going into the situation, the better you are likely to do, and once you achieve a positive result, it will reinforce your ability to achieve, which will help next time and so on, until you reach your final goal.

Humour

The final word in this chapter is on humour. When things are difficult and stressful, it can be difficult to keep a senses of humour, but being able to do this has kept me sane. I have found being dyslexic at times frustrating and stressful and on occasion depressing, and there have been times when trying to learn something, whilst having this constant barrier, has seemed hopeless. However, being dyslexic can also provide great humour. My misuse of words has been humorous on a number of occasions. I once wrote what I thought was a romantic letter, but confused the word 'dessert' with 'desert' and so effectively told my partner that I loved him like 'puddings' missed the rain. Text conversations can be both confusing and funny in equal measure, sometimes just one letter difference can change the meaning completely.

Being able to laugh at yourself and the situation can defuse tension and help to put things into perspective. Although I enjoy visual and surreal humour (Eddie Izzard, also dyslexic, being one of my favourite stand-up comedians), I will also watch comedians who use a lot of word play and puns (e.g. Tim Vine). Although I don't usually get the humour, I do this for educative purposes – if I only understand one meaning I will ask or find out what the other meaning is and, although this delay can negate the humour, it increases my knowledge of words and their meanings.

Chapter 10

Conclusion (What Have I Learnt so Far?)

Don't panic

When faced with a difficulty in learning, be it an exam, reading a document during class, for homework or solving a difficult puzzle, the first thing I have to remember is not to panic.

This may sound obvious, but if I start to think about how hard it will be, that I might look stupid if I get it wrong and about any negative past experiences, I will panic.

When my brain is spending all its energy and focus in panic mode, I cannot concentrate on the task in hand.

You could, like me, try taking some slow deep breaths to calm yourself. Or you could ask yourself, 'What is the worst that can happen if I get it wrong? Will anyone actually die?' (If you are a doctor or surgeon or work in a nuclear plant, it's probably best not to ask this!)

Love your brain

Learn to love the brain you have. My brain is working in a fundamentally different way to the brains of people who have no signs of dyslexia. This means that some tasks that are 'easy' or 'straightforward' for the non-dyslexic brain, will take me a long time or require some sort of support in order to be completed. However, this also means that my brain can make connections that a non-dyslexic brain may miss or overlook. A non-dyslexic brain may be unable to visualise ideas and solutions that can be a natural occurrence within a dyslexic (neuro-diverse) brain.

Scientists are beginning to recognise that if your brain solves problems using the fastest pathway (from a to b) to reach the solution, then the creative and innovative ideas will be lost. Creative thought requires following the meandering slower pathway to be able to reach more unusual and unique solutions.

Find the fun

Finding the fun in learning is the key to remembering what you have been taught. Humans are programmed to remember traumatic and horrible events (this is unfortunate), weird stuff and stuff that was fun.

So, if an elephant is brought into a lesson wearing an African headdress (weird), you will probably remember it. If the elephant has a 'little accident' in the class, you are even more likely to remember it (horrible), if the 'accident' in question happens on your shoes (traumatic) then you are unlikely to forget this, no matter how hard you try. Since most teachers and lecturers wouldn't want you to learn through traumatic experiences, the next best thing for your memory is for activities to be fun and interesting. Even the dullest content can be fun if delivered well.

Play games

You are never too old to play games. Some adults like to pretend that they are too old or sensible to play games, but you might later find out that they own a PlayStation, Xbox or Wii and are totally addicted to Grand Theft Auto, World of Warcraft or whatever is popular right now.

Even if the adult in question is from the pre-gaming generation (55 plus), they might have played Sudoku or completed a crossword at some time during the last week.

Games are good for us – they keep the brain actively engaged and can improve all kinds of mental abilities. Playing memory, word and number games (online or with real, as opposed to virtual, friends) as often as possible is a good way to maintain or improve your skill levels.

Read a good book

If, like most dyslexics (me included), you find the act of reading difficult because of moving words on the page, unfamiliar words or having to reread everything because the meaning didn't quite 'go in' the first time, then this might be the first thing you've read in a long time. (If that's true then, first of all, 'thanks' for choosing to read this and, second, 'congratulations'.)

Please don't give up on reading – even if it sometimes makes you want to bang your head against a wall – because there are some amazing books out there (yes, even better than this one!).

So, try different coloured backgrounds (reading rulers) or audio options (Read&Write Gold), large font, electronic reading pens or whatever it takes to stop you missing out, and maybe you will be the one writing books next.

Minimise stress

Many learning and assessment situations can be stressful; not understanding something completely, or not getting it right the first time can be frustrating. Anyone who struggles with the tasks of reading and writing can feel that their time and effort is often not rewarded with positive results in the learning environment.

Stress can have a negative effect on both mental and physical health, so finding ways to reduce stress is important.

Here are some of the methods I have used to counteract stress in learning:

- Taking regular breaks, even if you feel pushed for time. Remember, the human brain can have ideas and come up with solutions even when the problem isn't being consciously thought about.

- Exercise reduces levels of the stress hormone (cortisol) and can be very enjoyable if you find something you like.

- Creativity – doing something creative can increase positive thoughts and feelings and can therefore have a good impact on learning and life in general.

- Visualisations – these are not suitable for everyone and tend to work best with people who are predominantly visual thinkers (think in pictures) and imaginative (both qualities possessed by most dyslexics).

- Humour – it is difficult to stay stressed about something when you are laughing out loud.

Ask questions

<u>There is no such thing as a stupid question!</u>
I have underlined this because it is essential to remember this in learning. Curiosity is the reason most people want to learn: 'I wonder what happens if I...', 'I wonder how or why this works' or 'I wonder how much power the government really has.' The question could be anything, because it makes you want to find out more. A teacher may not like a question asked for one of two main reasons:

- They don't know the answer – we are all human and unless your teacher is some kind of rare genius they won't know all the answers. But it's very easy to look things up quickly these days (using the internet), so finding out isn't an issue.

- They don't think it's relevant – it might not be in that moment, or even for that session, but it might be something that will come up later, so it will be a good question to revisit later on.

My main goal as a learner is to have an understanding of the content, and as a tutor to assist the understanding of my learners. If no one asks a question, I may assume that everyone understands what we have covered, so be the brave person who asks what everyone else is probably thinking anyway.

Mind map your way to exam success

It has taken me over 20 years to get to a point where I don't have a complete meltdown about the idea of sitting an exam. Whilst I still feel a bit nervous just before the exam, I no longer let it take over my life in the weeks before it, reduce me to tears or nausea and lead me to feel that I am unable to cope with the pressure.

However, what is even more surprising than my altered attitude towards exams, is that my results have improved dramatically. In 2013 I took two Level 3 anatomy and physiology exams and achieved 100 per cent in both. This is amazing considering that I dropped biology in school in my third year.

So, what's my secret? Quite simply, mind maps (see Chapter 4). I find out what information or content is likely to be covered in the exam (teachers/tutors will normally guide you on this). Then I use the information to create an A3-size mind map, using lots of colours and images (I also like to use one colour per sub-topic, e.g. pink for muscles, purple for the nervous system, etc.). I then put up the mind maps on the walls around my house and spend 10–20 minutes a day just looking at them – not trying to remember them – just looking. I then ask someone to test me about three days later to identify any gaps. I continue to look at the mind maps, especially any parts I may have missed. Once in the exam, I remember colours, images and so on that linked directly to the information I want to retrieve.

Embrace challenges

This might sound like an odd piece of advice. Why not just enjoy the things you're good at and forget about doing things that you find difficult or challenging?

The reason is that, as human beings, when we are taking in new information or skills we follow a learning curve. This curve may alter from person to person, but what it means is that in the process of learning, some aspects will be more challenging than others and, during these challenging parts, persistence is key to achieving the final goal.

After the first three weeks of anatomy and physiology, I thought that my brain might explode (obviously we hadn't studied the brain at this stage, so I still thought this was possible!). The point is – I was struggling to keep up with an information overload and wondering what the hell I was thinking when I chose to do the course, and I was on the verge of giving up.

Luckily for me, I am quite stubborn and find it difficult to give anything up (it took six years to admit that playing the violin had beaten me), so I stuck with anatomy and physiology and, not only did it get easier as we began to cover slightly more familiar ground, but I also found I was starting to enjoy the course.

Celebrate

Celebrate success in learning in whatever form – whether it is learning a new language, an academic qualification or playing the drums, be proud and celebrate your achievements. We are all unique individuals with a variety of strengths, all of which are needed to make up the world. So feel free to give yourself a gold star just for being you.

Chapter 11

Kit and Caboodle

Useful websites
Dyslexia

American Dyslexia Association
www.american-dyslexia-association.com

Australian Dyslexia Association
www.dyslexiaassociation.org.au

British Dyslexia Association
www.bdadyslexia.org.uk

Canadian Dyslexia Association
www.dyslexiaassociation.ca

Dyslexia Research Trust
www.dyslexic.org.uk

Dyslexia Action
www.dyslexiaaction.org.uk

Dyslexia diagnosis and assessment

British Dyslexia Association
www.bdadyslexia.org.uk/dyslexic/
getting-an-assessment-for-dyslexia#Full
Diagnositc Assessments

'Dyslexia – Diagnosis'
NHS Choices
www.nhs.uk/Conditions/Dyslexia/
Pages/Diagnosis.aspx

'Getting your child assessed'
Dyslexia Action
www.dyslexiaaction.org.uk/
getting-your-child-assessed

Dyscalculia

**Conferences (for teachers) and
resources on dyscalculia**
www.dyscalculia.org

Irlen Syndrome

Irlen
www.irlen.org.uk

Irlen Centres
www.irlenuk.com

The Irlen Institute
www.irlen.com

Mind maps
**'Maximize the Power of Your Brain'
by Tony Buzan (YouTube video on
how to make a mind map)**
www.youtube.com/watch?v=MlabrWv25qQ

Brain-related information
'Amygdala'
About.com
http://biology.about.com/od/
anatomy/p/Amygdala.htm

**Physical Activity and Mental Health leaflet
from the Royal College of Psychiatrists**
www.rcpsych.ac.uk/healthadvice/
treatmentswellbeing/physicalactivity.aspx

Free online memory games
Play Pairs
www.web-games-online.com/
memory/index.php

PrimaryGames
www.primarygames.com

Dress Up Gal
www.dressupgal.com

Free online word games

Play Scrabble
www.memory-improvement-tips.com
/scrabble-online-free.html

Play Scrabble against online players
www.quadplex.com

How to play Pass the Bomb
www.word-buff.com/pass-the-bomb.html

Play Boggle
www.wordplays.com/boggle

Free online number games

Spiked Math Comics
www.spikedmath.com

Play Batters Up Baseball
www.prongo.com/math

Play Bubble Math
www.funnygames.co.uk/battle-math.htm

Stuff to buy/download

**Electronic reading pen: C-Pen
3.5 USB digital highlighter**
www.dyslexic.com

Quicktionary 2
www.scanningpenshop.com

**Reading rulers (variety of colours) and
educational games (word puzzles, etc.)**
www.crossboweducation.com

Read&Write Gold software
www.texthelp.com

Coggle
www.coggle.it

Any.do task and to-do list app
www.any.do

Books

Bird, R. (2013) *The Dyscalculia Toolkit*. London: SAGE Publications.

Davis, R. D. (1994) *The Gift of Dyslexia*. London: Souvenir Press.

Elliott, E. (2008) *Back to the Sky: How to Fly with Dyslexia*. London: Olympia Publishers.

Foer, J. (2011) *Moonwalking with Einstein: The Art and Science of Remembering Everything*. London: Penguin Books.

Wolf, M. (2008) *Proust and the Squid: The Story and Science of the Reading Brain*. London: Icon Books.

References

British Dyslexia Association (n.d.) *Dyscalculia*. UK: Bracknell: British Dyslexia Association. Available at www.bdadyslexia.org.uk/dyslexic/dyscalculia, accessed on 15 January 2015.

British Dyslexia Association (n.d.) *Getting an Assessment for Dyslexia*. UK: British Dyslexia Association. Available at www.bdadyslexia.org.uk/dyslexic/getting-an-assessment-for-dyslexia#Full Diagnostic Assessments, accessed on 26 November 2014.

Davis, R. D. (1994) *The Gift of Dyslexia*. London: Souvenir Press.

Dyslexia Research Trust (n.d.) *Vision and Coloured Filters*. Oxford: Dyslexia Research Trust. Available at www.dyslexic.org.uk/research/vision-coloured-filters, accessed on 15 January 2015.

Foer, J. (2011) *Moonwalking with Einstein: The Art and Science of Remembering Everything.* London: Penguin Books.

Gray, R. and Russell, P. (2012) 'Regular exercise can improve memory and learning.' *The Telegraph*, 19 February 2012. Available at www.telegraph.co.uk/health/healthnews/9090981/Regular-exercise-can-improve-memory-and-learning.html, accessed on 15 January 2015.

Law, S (2012) 'A brief history of numbers and counting, Part 1: Mathematics advanced with civilization.' *Deseret News*, 5 August 2012. Available at www.deseretnews.com/article/865560110/A-brief-history-of-numbers-and-counting-Part-1-Mathematics-advanced-with-civilization.html, accessed on 15 January 2015.

Sample, I (2010) 'Start running and watch your brain grow, say scientists.' *The Guardian*, 18 January 2010. Available at www.theguardian.com/science/2010/jan/18/running-brain-memory-cell-growth, accessed on 15 January 2015.

Wolf, M. (2008) *Proust and the Squid: The Story and Science of the Reading Brain.* London: Icon Books.

Index